THE TIMELESS WHEEL

Poems
by Adam Loeb

HATS
OFF

The Timeless Wheel
Copyright © 2001 Adam Loeb
All rights reserved. No part of this book may be reproduced or transmitted in any form or by any means without the written consent of the publisher.

Published by Hats Off Books™
610 East Delano Street, Suite 104
Tucson, Arizona 85705
www.HatsOffBooks.com
ISBN: 1-58736-053-5
LCCN: 2001090548
Book design by Summer Mullins
Printed in the United States of America.

DEDICATION

This book is dedicated to my glorious Indwelling Spirit,
my parents, Harvey and Sheila,
and to all proponents of peace.

CONTENTS

Acknowledgments 9

Preface 11

A Natural Feeling 13
Angels of Mercy 15
Ascension 17
Creator Son 19
Doves Take Flight 21
Dreaming 23
Forever 25
Forgotten Tears 27
Forward Always 29
Freedom Now 31
Freedom Road 33
Grandpa 35
Home 37
I Sing 39
Infinite Embrace 41
Kindred Spirit 43
Let your Mind Awake 45
Liberation 47
Light and Life 49
Looking Back 51
Martin 53
Mother Be Strong 55
Musical Inspiration 57
My Father 59
Nilsa 61
Nothing but Lies 63
Paradise Awaits 65
Precious 67
Prophecy 69

Revelation	71
Sage of Salem	73
Sharing	75
Singularity	77
Soul Song	79
Soul Survival	81
Spiritual Progress	83
Spring Time	85
The Family Endures	87
The Gift	89
The Greatest Mystery	91
The Healing	93
Together	95
Where Shall We Go	97
Where There is Love	99

ACKNOWLEDGMENTS

The following have my gratitude:

my father, who helped fortify the poems with his insight and knowledge;

my mother, for her kindness and support;

and The Urantia Book, *which taught me truth, beauty, and goodness.*

PREFACE

I believe that poetry is a path to enlighten and comfort those who are seeking the truth. This is my way of sharing my inner life with my fellows. In order for mankind to progress to a higher level, spirituality must pervade all aspects of our lives. Thoughts and actions of a reverent nature are instantaneously transmitted to the Universal Father.

A NATURAL FEELING

The greenness of nature is replenished
by the warm energy beyond the clouds.
As day turns into a nocturnal vibration,
the waves crash on the distant shore.
Beauty abounds,
the whispering wind glides
through my fingers.
With my eyes half-closed,
the starlight flashes toward me
and fills my heart with joy.

ANGELS OF MERCY

Gentle rain
descends from the mountains
as the dawn becomes
the morning.
Closing our eyes,
tuning out racing thoughts,
we are surrounded by
spirit energies,
angels of mercy.
These spirit beings,
a gift from the Infinite Spirit,
embrace our souls
as we leave this earth.

In the mansions of heaven
among the stars
we meet again
our indwelling spirit.
We are truly born again
and venture forth
to do His will
in the infinite cosmos.

ASCENSION

The Infinite Spirit downsteps the universes,
descending to Earth,
enhancing our minds,
teaching us wisdom and worship.
Our souls yearn for spiritual guidance
led by the indwelling spirit of God.
We are uplifted.
The sorrows of yesterday
pass away like dreams on
the river of time.
We live in the present moment
in prayer and meditation,
giving loving service to our fellows.

One day our souls will leave this place
and begin that great adventure,
ascending from sphere to sphere,
inhabiting the heavenly mansions
that reach across the stars
to the abode of the First Source and Center,
the eternal isle of Paradise.

CREATOR SON

Jesus of Nazareth, human and divine,
your matchless personality inspires me
and fills me with wonder.
I reach toward you
like a plant stretching toward the light
beyond the clouds.
If all men followed your teaching
peace on earth would prevail.
The Spirit of Truth which you
showered upon mankind
is reflected in the glowing eyes
of your children.
The leading of the Indwelling Spirit
is like the gusting wind,
carrying the righteous sailor
to lands of freedom.
Worlds without end,
and everlasting life.

DOVES TAKE FLIGHT

As the moonlight
fades into the
shadows of the night,
the clouds disperse
and the sun appears.
I awaken on a new shore.
Spirit beings embrace me
and doves take flight.
I am centered, able to see clearly,
like a hawk perched on a firm branch.
My senses have sharpened,
the invisible becomes visible.
The greatest adventure is before me:
to be perfect, even as
God is perfect.

DREAMING

I see ancient and
remembered time,
a mission sublime
to uplift mankind.
I see a garden of finest herbs
and sweetest fruits,
where love and peace abound.
A child sitting in a reverie
envisions an emerald timeless wheel,
exquisitely balanced.
Spirit gravity draws them inward
all souls connecting in friendship
like the cliff water
flowing effortlessly
into the starlit lake.

FOREVER

Starlight reflected by the mirror
propels beams,
rebounding off walls,
igniting candles in the incense filled room.

The ghostly circular motion of the smoke
and dancing shadows on the walls
draws me deep into a mood
where time is irrelevant.

Standing by Caribbean waters,
the illumination from the full moon
creates a soft delicate pattern
from the horizon
to my shadow.
The amorphous lunar glow
begins to sculpt beautiful soft curves of flesh,
and mysterious eyes.
Her sublime innocence,
subtle lips,
graceful style,
and warm sensitive touch
embody a private utopia.

She glides swiftly down the gleam of light
toward my soul,
a cosmic connection.
Two energies, who loved once on earth,
are able to find each other
outside the boundaries of material perception.

FORGOTTEN TEARS

Forgotten tears fill the ocean
like memories in the twilight wind.
The cries of the children go unheeded;
profit is the driving force
by any means necessary.
The war machine grinds inexorably.
Ecosystems are precarious.
Have courage, righteous men,
Spirit intelligences are among us.
They will teach us to
leave our wills behind and
follow the Divine Spirit.
As we drift up into the clouds
that quench the thirst of the vast trees,
the children's eyes will be filled with joy
and faith for a new morning,
a brighter day,
a cherished year,
a loving embrace.

FORWARD ALWAYS

Famished cries,
lonely eyes,
politicians' lies,
the cycle of poverty,
the dreams of liberty;
leaders of the peoples' struggles
gather their strength
in the silent night,
always spiritually right
with unity's might.

FREEDOM NOW

My heart is saddened by
forgotten children,
war and destruction.
Rulers of Babylon,
your days are numbered;
swept away
like sand castles and leaves in the wind.

Love is the way;
love another human today.
We who love peace
shall inherit the earth.
A new age will begin;
a spiritual age
of enlightenment and freedom.

FREEDOM ROAD

I hear the sound of a watch
keeping time into eternity.
The infinite cosmos awaits us.
My fears have disappeared,
I am within the sacred temple,
turning my will and my life
over to the care of God.

This is true Freedom,
my spiritual awakening.
As the Spirit quickens,
I become more humble,
spreading goodness and love.
I am walking the freedom road,
the pathway of infinite perfection.

GRANDPA

You are always in my heart.
As a child, remembering the anticipation
of those special visits,
kissing and hugging you and Grandma
filled me with the happiness of childhood.
I loved to climb the apple tree
in the backyard.
Grandma's beautiful artwork
filled the rooms with color
and expression of beauty and nature.
The sweet smell of your pipe tobacco
and the enticing aroma of
Grandma's delicious cooking
were days of wonder
making the rain stop,
the clouds disperse,
and the sun shine.

Grandpa was a wise man; he gave me
guidance and encouragement
to accomplish my objectives.
I know that one day
I will meet him again in the heavens
and our energies will connect in friendship.

HOME

A peaceful man
waves from the boat
on an endless journey of peace.
We will all learn to abide.
The moon is glowing so bright,
the stars directing the flight,
beyond the waves
and to the shore
of a higher land.
I stand on this foundation,
which is rocking so gently
beneath me
like a cradle.
It is Zion,
it must be, it
feels exactly like home.

I SING

I sing a song of love
and cherished times to come.
I sing this song of freedom
to abolish all oppression.
I sing this song
for poor man's redemption,
when racism will end
and love for every color will begin.
As I am singing,
the bells of peace are ringing.

INFINITE EMBRACE

Her beauty enraptures
my innocent youth.
A flowing nature embraces
lovely hair gliding like
the gentle wind on a warm spring day,
entering deep within my soul.
Her benign stare
makes me feel secure.
She is imprinted
upon the liquid in my eyes.

Tears of life fall,
carrying a part of her
and pieces of my personality
into the morning mist.
This is the affinity,
the dream,
the reality of being.

KINDRED SPIRIT

Hearing the waves
rolling toward the shoreline,
the movement of the ocean
is like the heartbeat of the earth,
the source of immense energy
illuminating the senses.
Your beauty enlightens me
in this special way.
Your precious stare
and loving affinity
fill my soul with love and joy.
As our eyes meet, we hear
the myriad sounds
of the night.
In the glimmering moonlight,
our minds connect,
flowing into each other
like the sands of time.

LET YOUR MIND AWAKE

Let your mind awake
and follow a falcon spreading its wings
for a journey
into a land of conflict and death.
Enter a desolate, ghostly town
trapped in a nocturnal abyss.
The circular motion of the wind
causes red dust
to assume macabre shapes.

The power of the vivid mind unites
with the spirit of nature and sees
the piercing lighting blaze through the dense clouds
illuminating the forces of good and evil in conflict.
Let the clouds disperse until rays of pure energy warm the earth.
As day turns into night,
a gentle zephyr soothes the soul
and the sky sparkles with stars.
Let the choking earth breathe once again
and not be destroyed by pollutants, violence and greed.

In the empty arid town,
a raindrop touches my powerful mystic eyes.
I drift into my unconsciousness;
vivid images of revelation
present a solution
by challenging the unrighteous.

Poetry glows,
a transformation of energy from
my abstract thoughts
through your body, entering your mind.
We must unite,
the poetry will be our tool.
As I awake in this strange town,
the sun rises and sets like time passing.
We must seize the time.

LIBERATION

Strive for a true democracy
where reality is seen
through the eyes of the beholder
who knows the truth
which has been revealed by the Sons of God.
Until the philosophy of peaceful unification
is concretized,
we must fight for equal rights and justice.
Unite in this time of strife,
until love and unity abound.
When men are free
to decide their own destiny,
Democracy will finally
become a reality.

LIGHT AND LIFE

Our heritage is peace,
a brotherhood of man
shining in the blue sky
and among the clouds.
Peace begins in the family,
the basic unit of human society.
The family builds a foundation of love,
spreading out to the schools,
the communities,
the nations;
one human family,
holding hands across the sea.

LOOKING BACK

Standing alone,
waves approaching,
the sun rises to the left of the lighthouse,
and the sand flows into the ocean.
On this warm sunlit day,
watching dolphins play,
thinking of the times with my friends
close to Harlem nights:
Jazz music filled the air,
candlelight flickering in the night,
dancing shadows poised in flight.

Standing alone again
the waves touch my feet,
I sense the presence of spirits
everywhere;
guiding my mind,
soothing my soul,
and I know
I am not alone.

MARTIN

He was a man among men
doing God's will,
bringing people together
in peace and friendship,
one human family.
We stand with King
with arms linked
challenging evil.

For the love of God,
for the love of each other,
we are faithful sons,
we will prevail.

MOTHER BE STRONG

You, who brings life into the world,
you must be saved from trouble and war.
Mother, hiding your tears,
you deserve an endless time
of freedom and love.
Mother, in time all will be revealed.
You will discover the everlasting Power within yourself.
This living water will quench your thirst
for serenity and joy.
As you give of yourself
to your children,
spirit personalities are drawn to you
and they rejoice.
Mother, your unique nature
is like rainbow colors blended
into strong clay
by the fiery sun.
Mother, as your years pass,
do not be concerned,
for this life is the stepping stone
into eternity.

MUSICAL INSPIRATION

My music is mellow,
the tone from my saxophone
fills the air with clarity.
My rhythm flows
like waves raising up
toward the sky,
and returning to the endless seas,
where there are no trees,
only the horizon and gigantic clipper ships
sailing adrift
on open waters,
exploring new lands,
new skies,
riding the tides.
Music brings peace to my soul
taking me deep within.
The racing thoughts are quiet
and I perceive spiritual presence
vibrating with love,
the pure music of my salvation.

MY FATHER

You are awesome and mysterious,
giving my life meaning.
You shine with an inner light,
intriguing, like the eclipse of the moon.
You are always present for me,
like the stars in the sky, your love will never die.
Our lives are intertwined forever.
We shall overcome all adversity
and be free for all eternity
in the hands of the Universal Father,
The Lord of Peace.

NILSA

Humming and singing
child of the world,
trapped in a smoke-filled room
breathing a cloud of corruption and greed,
which pollutes the air for the sake of profit.
Leave that space
and find a place
of serenity and grace
where birds and flowers,
all nature's creations,
live in balance
in the pure air of life.

NOTHING BUT LIES

Her enraptured sunlit eyes
penetrate the skies
revealing the lies upon the earth.
The truth exists beyond
the whispering signs of deception
and generates a feeling of hope
to be fulfilled.
Positive vibrations of a nation
moving toward revelation
and the renewal of God's creation.

PARADISE AWAITS

The Lord's Prayer
no fear
only whispered cheers
from the silent night
and the sunny day
warming the waters
that caress
the moon-lit river bank.

Tomorrow's endless tears
will fade away.
Surrounded by heavens grace,
ascending from mansion to mansion,
angels lead us to our destiny.

Creation surrounds us
as we soar forever inward
transcending the flesh.
Spirit beings we become,
Paradise before us;
behold our God.

PRECIOUS

Precious Angel,
you brighten my day with
radiance like a full lunar glow.
You are like a beam of starlight
gliding through the sky,
filling my soul with joy and beauty.
The caterpillar awaits the time
to become a colorful spectrum
blended in your darling eyes.
We soar high in the windy sky
hearing nothing but the
beating of our hearts.
You are the precious mentor
that carries me ever inward
to the First Source and Center.

PROPHECY

And the prophets told of a new world to come
when swords shall be beaten into plowshares
and nations shall war no more.
Our planet shall become a realm of love,
joy and laughter abounding.
Peaceful butterflies of myriad colors,
flowers gently blooming,
creating pollen for busy bees.
Serenity is forever enhanced.
Pure sunlight envelops us,
bringing food for the birds,
giving them strength to take flight,
majestic trees protecting them
from thunderstorms.
Sounds ring forth in the streets
to liven the lives of men and women
full of humility and doing the will
of the Father.
They learn the secrets of nature
and food will be abundant
throughout the ghettos and third world countries.
Angelic song, heard by the children,
echoes in the heavens
as the celestial hosts rejoice.
Every soul on earth will be led to the moon river
just over the mountains,
where the tree of life replenishes the heavenly ones.
The tear-filled ocean will evaporate
and fear will disappear.

REVELATION

The days bring me joy.
Rays of light
penetrate my soul with delight
and memories fade
into the depths of the night.
Sorrows of the earth
fill my empty vessel with empathy.
Cries of the children will be heard
like thunderous voices in the wind;
and the flight of the mockingbird
leads to spirit forces
of the most High
to heal the nation
in this pure and true revelation.

SAGE OF SALEM

Machiventa Melchizedek,
sage of Salem;
your spiritual presence
down through the ages
has influenced the prophets
and taught man about God.
You are truly a prince of peace,
endeavoring to bring humanity
out of darkness and isolation.
Under your guidance
our destiny is alive and glowing.
Peace on earth,
endless dreams,
creativity abounds
and Seraphim are near,
ministering to us
with loving kindness.
A unified planetary government
is firmly established
and the universe circuits are open
connecting mankind to the living Cosmos.

SHARING

Great mysterious snowflakes,
the radiant ocean,
pearled moon full and bright,
reflect the power of creation,
the mystery of evolution.
As finite beings,
we are bound by these natural laws.
By sharing our inner life with God,
we show willingness to become god-like.
This is the key
that opens our minds to
the Spirit from above,
guiding us through
the uncertain maze of life.
Glorious Indwelling,
Everlasting Power,
you offer us this precious gift
of free will choice;
to love or to hate,
to preserve or destroy,
to survive or to perish.

SINGULARITY

We are like precious stones,
each one a unique personality
bestowed by the Father.
Look within the hearts of people
to find the spark of Divinity.
The brotherhood of man,
the Fatherhood of God,
that is all we need
to end chaos and war
and create a world of universal love and kindness
to one another.

SOUL SONG

Can we heal the wounds
of all the yesterdays?
Can we dance the freedom song
for all eternity?
Are we in balance
with nature,
the winter snowflakes,
the frozen pond,
the bare trees
in winter's embrace?

Give peace to your souls
and evil will not find you.
Give peace to your souls
and good will embrace you
and never let go.

SOUL SURVIVAL

Wickedness comes like
a thief in the night,
corrupting your mind,
robbing your soul.
Be careful what you learn,
be cautious who you obey.
On judgment day
your deeds will be reckoned.
It is time to choose the spiritual path
and make amends to those you have hurt.
Conscious evil brings non-existence.
Embracing love leads to soul survival.
The Universal Father is the divine pattern
for mercy and justice.
When we follow the leading
of the spirit from above,
He is filled with love for his earth children,
and we are his faith-sons forever.

SPIRITUAL PROGRESS

While I sojourn on this planet
I consider my dual nature;
a material being with my ego
bearing a precious gift from
my Heavenly Father,
the indwelling spirit.
If I follow his will
I become a spiritual person
getting involved in doing good,
respecting and loving my neighbor.
I hope my voice will be heard
by those who are oppressed.
The kingdom of heaven
is within you if you open your heart
and listen to the truth.
If every man would turn to another
and say "I love you,"
universal peace would reign.

SPRING TIME

Waking this morning
to the sound of the gentle wind
birds singing
trees swaying
the times changing.
Spring is here,
nature blooming
like daisies in a sunlit room.
My eyes reflect the vitality
and grace of nature.
Memories fill my mind.
True and beautiful friend
if only you were here
embracing me,
walking hand in hand
across fields of wild flowers.
My kindred spirit,
you are in my heart forever.
Together, we could face the confusion
and chaos of the times.
Wars and rumors of wars,
greed, corruption, and self-interest;
the time has come to hold hands
with our brothers and sisters,
faith-children of God
practicing those divine principles
of Truth, Beauty, and Goodness;
and this planet will rise out of isolation
and join the cosmic community
with the parts and the whole
functioning in Divine balance.

THE FAMILY ENDURES

There is love in my family
that goes beyond cruel words
and thoughtless deeds.
Please don't break the loving embrace
that shines through the tears.
The bond forged between us
gives meaning and strength of purpose to my life.
Forgiveness and acceptance,
brother to brother,
wife to husband,
will raise our connection to a new level,
a spiritual plane of existence.
A new life is awaiting
beyond the clouds.
In the presence of spirit intelligence,
our family will be drawn together,
and we will be closer
than the setting sun
as it touches the horizon.

THE GIFT

The spirit of truth
bestowed by the Master,
governs the enlightened ones
gently and perfectly
like moonlight,
luminescent on the glittering sea.

By embracing truth, beauty, and goodness,
we will be led to Jesus, Creator Son,
who taught us the truth;
the kingdom of heaven, within.

THE GREATEST MYSTERY

The Universal Father has offered,
with his loving and gentle heart,
a fragment of himself
to indwell in our minds,
leading us toward peace and harmony.
We are drawn like a magnet
inward, toward the center of creation,
meeting pilgrims from every universe
as we become spirit beings,
cosmic citizens,
connected to the heart of love,
the living cosmos.
We are becoming more and more perfect,
enhancing reality.

To dance the freedom song,
and stride the freedom road,
the path to infinity becomes clearer
and starlight illuminates the
way to Paradise.

THE HEALING

Revelation reveals the truth
of God's creation.
This illumination from the aura
will ignite the darkness,
teaching man to reach beyond the self,
going beyond our range of expectation
to heal the nation,
to save the Lord's creation
through peaceful revelation.

We seek a true democracy,
a world government
with equal rights and justice;
and all men will be free
to decide their own destiny.

TOGETHER

You are the light of my life;
you love and care for me
with boundless grace.
Have faith and courage
and remember the good times we shared.

We are kindred spirits;
our spiritual natures
exhibit an attractiveness,
a cohesiveness,
that will draw us together
in a future time and space.

WHERE SHALL WE GO?

Where shall we go
when the conflict grows?
Like the sparrow
We walk with our chins up
as they come
with their weapons of destruction.
We confront them
with pens held high.
Our pens glimmer
in their eyes
and they turn away,
never to cross the lake
where we build our homes
and grow our crops.
We welcome the rain
that always seems to come on time,
sustaining us,
as the sun rises in the east,
so effortless,
so pure.

WHERE THERE IS LOVE

Love is the most powerful force
bestowed by the Universal Father
upon the worlds of time and space.
Where there is love,
no need to fight,
no time for war,
tribulation and strife.
Love is beautiful and mysterious,
like the rainbow connecting
the earth to the sky.
Where there is love
faith will come
in its dewy morning,
like the mountains that soar through the clouds,
past the rising sun
to the stars.
Love is nature,
its beauty illuminates our eyes
and guides our path toward enlightenment.
With love we will always move forward
and we shall be free
like the birds that
traverse the sea
and the waves that break gently
on the shoreline,
because love is always on time.